The Universal Spiritual Laws

A Poetry Journey

By

Shreeya Sharma

INDIA • SINGAPORE • MALAYSIA

ISBN

Hardcase 979-8-89961-988-5
Paperback 979-8-89961-987-8

The Universal Spiritual Laws — A Poetry Journey

This book is a work of creative spiritual reflection. While rooted in ancient and universal principles, the poems and interpretations herein are original expressions by the author and are not affiliated with any religious institution.

For permissions, inquiries, or rights, contact:
shreeya.sharma@hotmail.com

ISBN:

Hardcase 979-8-89961-988-5
Paperback 979-8-89961-987-8

Cover Art and Illustrations:
AI-generated and curated by the author
Book Design: Ar. Shreeya Sharma

Printed in India
First Edition, 2025

Dedicated to

"To the Light in all things—may you remember yourself."

"What you are, you radiate. What you radiate, you attract. What you attract, teaches you."

"You are not lost — you are **unlearning who you were told to be.** *This in-between time is sacred. Don't fill it too quickly. Listen to the whisper behind the restlessness — it holds the map."*

– Shreeya S.

Contents

Acknowledgments

To the Divine intelligence that weaves through everything — thank you for allowing me to remember, receive, and record what flows through silence.

To the ancient seers, sages, and spiritual traditions — especially the Vedic rishis — who whispered these truths long before we had names for them, your resonance still echoes through every verse.

To my family and friends, inner circle of love and light — thank you for holding space while I disappeared into devotion. For every moment of stillness you supported, for every silence you understood.

To my readers — whether you stumbled here or were guided — thank you for listening with your heart. This book is as much yours as it is mine.

To the Earth, whose rhythm pulses beneath each word.
To the breath, that carried the wisdom in.
To the mystery, for never fully revealing itself.

With deepest gratitude,
Shreeya S.

Preface

There are laws more subtle than gravity — laws not written in books or courts, but in the breath of the universe itself. These spiritual laws govern not only the shape of stars, but the shape of our becoming.

This book is not a manual. It is a mirror. A collection of poems that reflect the invisible truths woven into every moment of our lives. Each law here is not a rule to follow, but a frequency to align with — a way of remembering what your soul already knows.

I did not write this book to teach. I wrote it to transmit — insight, presence, and resonance. To invite you into deeper awareness, not through instruction, but through vibration. These verses were born of silence, contemplation, and the deep listening that happens when one sits with truth long enough for it to speak.

You do not need to read this book in order. You may read one poem and let it echo for days. Or move through the laws in sequence, as a path of unfolding. Let intuition be your compass.

May these words not only explain — but awaken.

With love and light,
Shreeya

Introduction: The Eternal Laws of Life

In the vast expanse of existence, certain principles remain constant—guiding forces that, though unseen, shape the rhythm of the cosmos and the journey of every soul. These are the **Universal Spiritual Laws**, timeless truths that govern the interplay between the inner self and the external world.

Roots in Ancient Wisdom

The concept of universal laws is deeply embedded in the spiritual traditions of India. The **Vedas**, among the oldest sacred texts, introduce foundational principles like *Rta (रत)*—the cosmic order that maintains harmony in the universe.

Building upon this, the **Upanishads** delve into the nature of reality and the self. They teach that beneath the transient world lies the *Atman*, the true self, which is identical to *Brahman*, the ultimate reality. Recognizing this unity is essential for liberation.

The **Bhagavad Gita**, a dialogue between Prince Arjuna and Lord Krishna, further elucidates these laws, emphasizing the importance of *Dharma* (righteous duty), *Karma* (action and its consequences), and *Bhakti* (devotion) in achieving spiritual fulfilment.

Navigating Life Through Universal Laws

These spiritual laws are not abstract doctrines but practical guides for daily living:

- **Law of Karma**: Every action has consequences. Understanding this encourages mindful living and personal responsibility.
- **Law of Dharma**: Each individual has a unique purpose. Aligning with one's dharma leads to fulfillment and harmony.
- **Law of Detachment**: Letting go of attachment to outcomes fosters inner peace and resilience.
- **Law of Unity**: Recognizing the interconnectedness of all beings cultivates compassion and empathy.

By internalizing these principles, one can navigate life's challenges with clarity and grace, transforming obstacles into opportunities for growth.

A Journey Inward

This book is an invitation to explore these universal laws through poetic reflections. Each poem serves as a mirror, reflecting the truths that reside within and around us. As you engage with these verses, may you uncover the wisdom that guides your path and the light that illuminates your soul.

Understanding Energy: A Note to the Reader

We often hear: "Everything is energy." But what does that truly mean?

Energy is not some abstract force floating in the cosmos — it is the language of the universe. Before words, before form, before matter, there is vibration. There is frequency. There is intention. And the universe listens.

Unlike the co-existing dualities we live in — good and bad, light and dark, more and less — energy is binary at its core. To the universe, things either *exist* or they *do not.* It responds not to what we want, but to what we *are.* Not to what we say once, but to what we continuously *vibrate.*

In this way, your thoughts are code. Your emotions are signals. Your beliefs are programming. You are constantly broadcasting information, and the universe, in return, rearranges itself to match your signal — without judgment, delay, or exception.

There is no morality in this response. It is not personal. It is precise.

So as you begin to explore these spiritual laws — understand this:

You are not asking the universe to give.
You are telling it what to mirror.

Speak consciously.
Think intentionally.
Feel truthfully.
Choose powerfully.

Because energy doesn't lie.
And reality listens.

Part I – The Basic Laws of Life

Foundation of spiritual navigation — how your inner world creates your outer experience.

These laws teach that life is a mirror of your internal state. Your thoughts, feelings, beliefs, and energy constantly broadcast signals to the universe, attracting people, circumstances, and experiences into your life. The principles here—like the Law of Attraction, Reflection, Projection, and Attachment—reveal how deeply your reality is shaped by the energetic messages you emit and the emotional patterns you hold.

When you learn to request consciously, release resistance, and take responsibility for your vibrational signature, you begin to transform your lived reality from the inside out. This section invites you to become aware of what you're broadcasting—and to reclaim authorship over your life by shifting your internal dialogue.

THE BASIC LAWS OF LIFE

A foundational meditation on life's invisible architecture.

1.

The soul does not drift —
it draws.
Every person, moment,
and shadow
enters at invitation,
silent, but not accidental.

2.

Life is made of mirrors.
We ask, it answers.
We push, it pushes.
We resist, it remains.
We open — and it becomes wind.

3.

You do not walk through a world —
you build it as you breathe.
Each belief a blueprint,
Each emotion, mortar.
You live in a temple
you cannot see.

4.

There are no random events.
Only unconscious prayers
answered
perfectly.

5.

The laws are not punishment
nor reward.
They are truth
rising to meet
the shape
you've made of yourself.

The Law of Attraction

You are a living magnet — constantly attracting into your life the people, experiences, and situations that match your dominant thoughts and emotional frequency. Your outer reality reflects your inner landscape. Whether consciously or unconsciously, every belief and vibration you hold is broadcasting a message to the universe. When you change your internal narrative, your external circumstances shift to match. This law reminds you: like attracts like — and your life is the echo of your own energetic resonance.

Key concepts:

- Like attracts like; your thoughts, beliefs, and feelings emit a frequency that draws people and events into your life.
- Your body mirrors your inner emotional state.
- You unconsciously magnetize experiences that match your internal vibration — both positive and negative.
- To change your reality, change your inner thoughts and energy.

THE LAW OF ATTRACTION

"Like attracts like. You do not chase your life—you shape it."

1.
You are a field,
not a seeker.
The seeds you whisper
under breath
become forests
on your path.

2.
The body grows
around the heart's hidden words.
What you bury,
blossoms—
fat, muscle, ache,
or armor.

3.
Desperation prays in reverse.
It says:
"I do not have."
And so,
the law obeys.

4.
Everything that hurts you
came home to heal you.
It knew your name—
because you whispered it
long before it came.

5.
You don't pull in what you wish for—
only what you already believe.
Desire is wind.
Belief is gravity.

6.
Every complaint
is a command.
Every sigh
an instruction.

7.
The mirror does not judge.
It reflects
your truest tone.
Smile with doubt,
and it smiles back crooked.

8.
You attract the storm
not because you want pain—
but because the lightning matches
your frequency.

9.
You have drawn
each face you see
into your life—
not by will,
but by resonance.

10.
The words you never say
are the ones
the universe listens to most.
They hum beneath
your yes and no.

11.
The unspoken grief
becomes the partner.
The buried shame—
the job.
The secret joy—
a child,
a friend,
a miracle.

12.
It's not magic.
It's math.
Your vibration plus your pattern
equals your life.

13.

Be careful when you say:
"I don't want this."
The law only hears
"This."

14.

You don't get what you deserve.
You get what you match.
Raise your frequency—
and watch
what falls away.

15.

The future is not fate—
it's a mirror
tilted by belief.

16.

Need is loud
but not magnetic.
Stillness is quiet—
but it draws the whole sky.

17.

If you fear being alone,
you'll find the absent.
If you become content,
you'll attract presence.

18.
When you change the story
you tell your cells,
your body
changes its script.

19.
Love comes
when you love without needing.
Wealth comes
when you give with ease.
Everything
meets its match.

20.
Look at your life—
it is your broadcast,
made visible.

The Law of Request

In the spiritual realm, nothing intervenes without permission. The Law of Request teaches that divine help requires a conscious invitation. Angels, guides, and higher beings stand by ready to assist, but only when asked with sincerity and clarity. Likewise, human help must also be guided by respect — uninvited interference hinders growth. When your soul is ready to ask, it signals your readiness to receive.

Key concepts:

- Spiritual help must be asked for; no higher being interferes without permission.
- Clarity, readiness, and intention are required to receive guidance.
- Imposing help on others without consent causes karmic entanglement.
- Desperation blocks spiritual support; calm openness invites it.

THE LAW OF REQUEST

"You must ask, and ask from readiness—not from lack."

1.

Heaven waits
like a well-trained friend—
near enough to help,
but never uninvited.

2.

A prayer that begs
is not heard the same
as a prayer that opens.
The first is fear.
The second, trust.

3.

Help surrounds you—
but it cannot land
where there is no welcome.

4.

You must ask
not with desperation,
but with dignity.
Even angels honor consent.

5.

Every time you ask clearly,
the universe says:
"Now you are ready."

6.

Guidance waits
at the edge of your surrender.
It will not cross the threshold
until you do.

7.

It is not weakness
to ask for light.
It is how stars are born.

8.

Nothing is withheld.
Only unrequested.

9.

You block miracles
not by silence—
but by the pride that thinks
it must earn everything first.

10.

Do not rush to rescue.
Unasked help
is another form of control.

11.
Even the moon
waits for nightfall
to rise.

12.
When the soul asks,
the winds shift.
Even before the answer arrives.

13.
To impose is to interrupt
another soul's learning.
To assist without asking
is to claim their path as yours.

14.
A sincere request
is the unlocking
of karmic grace.

15.
The voice that wails "Why?"
is not the same
as the voice that whispers,
"What now?"

16.
The universe reads your energy,
not your words.
You cannot fake asking.

17.
To ask rightly
is to name
what you are willing to receive.

18.
Every unopened door
you curse—
you never knocked.

19.
Spiritual help is bound
by cosmic law.
It watches,
but does not enter
without your call.

20.
Ask, not as a beggar—
but as a co-creator
who has remembered
their inheritance.

The Law of Resistance

Whatever you resist, persists. Your unconscious cannot process negatives — it responds only to what you focus on. Thoughts like "I don't want to be ill" still attract illness, because 'ill' is what the energy is built around. Resistance amplifies what we fear. This law invites you to replace resistance with focus — not on what you don't want, but on what you're calling in.

Key concepts:

- Whatever you resist, persists; thinking about what you *don't* want magnetizes it.
- Victimhood and negative self-talk trigger resistance and attract more of what you avoid.
- Replace resistance with attraction to its opposite (e.g., focus on health, not avoiding illness).

THE LAW OF RESISTANCE

"What you push away, you call closer. What you resist, persists."

1.

The mind says, "Not this,"
but the soul knows—
you just gave it a name.
And so it comes.

2.

Every "I don't want"
is a magnet.
It calls the unwanted
by name.

3.

Resistance is prayer
written in reverse.

4.

Your fears don't listen
to logic.
They follow vibration—
and they obey repetition.

5.
You cannot escape
what you energize.
To fight a thing
is to feed it.

6.
The word "no"
does not exist
in the language
of the universe.

7.
Even illness bows
to your focus.
You say "I hate this body,"
and it tightens its ache
to hear you better.

8.
Resisting the fire
only scorches the hands.
Step back—
or let it burn through
what was never yours.

9.
Your "I won't be like them"
is the thread
that ties you to them.

10.
You cannot outrun
what you fear—
only outgrow it.

11.
The more you defend,
the more you declare
that you are under threat.

12.
What you avoid,
you invite.
Softly.
But surely.

13.
Your "no"
is a hidden obsession.
And obsession
is attraction
in disguise.

14.
The shadow grows
where attention hides.

15.
Do not shout at the mirror.
Change the face.

16.
A locked jaw,
a clenched fist,
a furrowed brow—
these are all doors
you're forcing open
against yourself.

17.
The path clears
not when you push,
but when you
stop pushing.

18.
Even "I must not fail"
is a script
written in fear
and handed
to your future.

19.
Say instead:
"I walk in ease."
And the burden
will forget
your name.

20.

Let go—
not to abandon,
but to transform
what clings
into what flows.

The Law of Reflection

The universe is a perfect mirror. Every person, situation, and pattern in your life reflects some aspect of your inner self — acknowledged or not. If something or someone triggers you, look within. The more intense the reaction, the deeper the mirror. Understanding this law dissolves blame and opens the door to profound self-awareness and growth.

Key concepts:

- Everyone and everything in your life is a mirror of some aspect of yourself.
- The more something bothers you in others, the more it reflects your unheealed traits.
- Your environment, animals, car, and surroundings reflect your energy and emotional state.

THE LAW OF REFLECTION

"Everything you meet is a mirror. Especially what you cannot accept."

1.
Life holds up a mirror—
not to mock,
but to show you
your shape in motion.

2.
Every face
is a silent teacher.
What you praise,
you are.
What you condemn,
you carry.

3.
If it triggers,
it teaches.
If it angers,
it reveals.

4.
You see cruelty—
are you healing yours?
You see beauty—
have you claimed it yet?

5.

The world does not happen
to you.
It happens
through you.

6.

Three mirrors come
when one won't wake you.
Water, fire, and stone—
emotion, energy, matter.
Each says:
"Look again."

7.

That friend who drains you
mirrors the part of you
that overgives
to feel loved.

8.

The person who ignores you
reflects the voice in you
you still ignore.

9.

The child who defies
shows you the parent in you
who's never been heard.

10.

When the car won't start,
ask:
Where have you stopped moving?

11.

If the lights go out—
can you see
where you've gone dim?

12.

Even the scratch
on your wall
is a whisper
from your restless mind.

13.

Your animals act out
what you bury.
Their peace is your peace.
Their growl—your guilt.

14.

Look again at the one
who irritates you.
They are only your wound
with a different face.

15.

The more it repeats,
the deeper the mirror.
Patterns are not curses—
they are lessons
not yet learned.

16.

Even clutter
is a reflection.
Of fear, of holding,
of what you won't release.

17.

You asked for clarity.
So life sent you
every version of yourself
you never wanted to meet.

18.

Don't ask, "Why is this here?"
Ask:
"What in me made space
for this guest?"

19.

Sometimes grace arrives
as discomfort—
a mirror held so close
you flinch before you thank it.

20.

When the lesson lands,
the mirror breaks.
And you find yourself
more whole
than before.

The Law of Projection

What we deny in ourselves, we project onto others. When we say "you are…", we often reveal what we refuse to claim within. Projection is a defense — it masks fear and prevents responsibility. But it also applies to our beauty: when we see greatness in others, we're recognizing a latent light in ourselves. This law asks us to own both shadow and shine.

Key concepts:

- You see your unacknowledged qualities in others — both negative and positive.
- Statements like "You are…" often reveal more about *you* than them.
- Projection is a form of denial and avoidance of self-responsibility.

THE LAW OF PROJECTION

"What you see outside, you placed there. Every judgment is a reflection in disguise."

1.
When you say,
"She is too much,"
you mean:
"I have not yet made peace
with my own bigness."

2.
Each "You are..."
is a window
into your own
unfinished sentence.

3.
We do not see people.
We see through them
into ourselves.

4.
Even your enemies
carry your fingerprints.

5.
Every accusation
is an autobiography
in disguise.

6.
You saw pride in her—
because your own confidence
still frightens you.

7.
We project to avoid.
We label
to delay healing.

8.
He cheated,
because you still suspect
you are not enough.

9.
The one who sees danger
in every shadow
is haunted
by their own.

10.
Before you correct the world,
ask:
What are you hiding
from yourself?

11.
"You must feel awful,"
you said—
because you would,
if you stood in their shoes.

12.
What you repress
becomes a lens
over every eye you meet.

13.
Projection
is perception
carrying baggage.

14.
You see betrayal everywhere—
but your trust
was broken by you
long before they did it.

15.
Even the praise you give
is a projection.
You see greatness—
because you carry it.

16.

The gentlest souls
are sometimes the most judged—
because gentleness
is still waiting
to be let in.

17.

If everyone seems cold,
check your walls.
You may have painted the world
with your frost.

18.

Those who shame others
fear their own shame
will be found.

19.

To see with clean eyes
is to strip away
the layers
you placed upon the world.

20.

The law is simple:
You cast the shadow,
then flinch
when it waves back.

The Law of Attachment

Attachment creates suffering. When your happiness, identity, or worth depends on something or someone, you become bound — energetically, emotionally, karmically. Attachment forms cords, which can persist across lifetimes. The more we try to control, the more entangled we become. This law invites you to release the need to possess — and discover the freedom of unconditional love.

Key concepts:

- You can enjoy people and things, but if your happiness depends on them, you are attached.
- Emotional cords form between people with unresolved issues; these can continue across lifetimes.
- Neediness and conditional love create entanglement; unconditional love releases.

THE LAW OF ATTACHMENT

"What you cling to, owns you. What you release, frees you."

1.

You can love deeply
without holding tightly.
Only fear wraps chains
around the heart.

2.

Need disguises itself
as love—
but real love breathes
without a leash.

3.

Whatever you *must* have
to feel whole
is the very thing
keeping you fragmented.

4.

You are allowed to own things.
But never let them
own your peace.

5.

Cords are not just felt—
they are fed.
Every grudge, craving, and guilt
adds another knot.

6.

Conditional love says:
"I love you, *if*..."
Unconditional love says:
"I am free,
and I see you are too."

7.

Co-dependence is not closeness—
it is closeness held hostage.

8.

You cling to the story
so tightly
that your hands forget
how to open.

9.

The fear of losing
creates the ache
that drives it away.

10.
True love arrives
when it knows
it can leave.

11.
Letting go
does not mean
losing.
It means you trust
that nothing real
can be lost.

12.
Attachments form cords.
Cords cross lifetimes.
What you refuse to forgive
you'll meet again.

13.
Your grief
is not for the person—
it's for the part of you
that still believes
you needed them to be okay.

14.
You trap yourself
every time you whisper,
"I can't live without..."

15.

Attachment wears the face
of concern, protection, loyalty—
but at its root
it is control
wrapped in longing.

16.

The house,
the role,
the name—
they are not *you*.
You existed
before the label.

17.

The more you let go,
the more flows in.
A closed fist
receives nothing.

18.

Some parents bind their children
so tightly
that neither grows.
Love is not a leash.

19.

Release isn't forgetting.
It's remembering who you are
without the chain.

20.

Say:
"I love you, and I free you."
Then watch
as peace
finally stays.

Part II – The Laws of Creation

How you shape reality through intention, clarity, and vibration.

These laws reveal that we are not passive recipients of life but powerful creators. By directing our attention, setting intentions, and cultivating clarity, we tune ourselves into the vibrational current of what we wish to receive. Abundance, manifestation, prosperity, and success are not luck—they are the results of aligned energy, belief, and self-trust.

This section emphasizes the energetic architecture behind results. The clearer your vision, the purer your intent, the more the universe conspires in your favor. When your inner frequency matches your desired outcome, creation flows naturally.

THE LAWS OF CREATION

A prelude to conscious crafting — of reality, purpose, and destiny.

1.

Creation is not an act—
it is a resonance.
You do not build the world
with hands,
but with the music
of your focus.

2.

Every outcome
starts as a whisper
in the field of attention.
To create is not to force—
but to tune.

3.

The Creator lives
within the created.
You are not outside the design.
You are the pen.
The sketch.
And the hand that draws.

4.

What you believe,
you begin.
What you sustain,
you become.
This is the holy cycle
of all manifestation.

5.

To create
is to say yes
to unseen forces
ready to shape themselves
in your name.

The Law of Attention

Where attention goes, energy flows. Every thought is a command. Whatever you continuously focus on — desired or feared — is magnetized into your life. This law teaches the power of mental discipline and intentional awareness. What you nourish with your attention will grow.

Key concepts:

- Energy flows where attention goes.
- You manifest exactly what you give focus to — fear, joy, health, etc.
- Positive focus strengthens dreams; worry empowers fears.

THE LAW OF ATTENTION

'Where your gaze rests, your life grows." Or "where attention goes, energy flows'

1.
What you water
with thought
will grow—even weeds.

2.
The universe is impartial—
it doesn't care
if you're focused on fear
or freedom.
It simply says:
"So be it."

3.
You are not trapped—
you are merely looking
in the same direction
for too long.

4.
The smallest worry,
when watched,
becomes a wall.

5.

Your attention
is a magnifying glass.
And the sun burns
whatever you place beneath it.

6.

You do not have to fight
every fear.
Just stop feeding it
your gaze.

7.

Miracles are not rare—
you just stopped
looking for them.

8.

To focus on the storm
is to miss
the lighthouse.

9.

If you wish to create
peace, joy, love—
look only
where they live.

10.
Even in stillness,
your thoughts are travelers.
And the soul follows
where they go.

11.
Every repetition
etches a groove
into the mind.
And then the soul walks it,
thinking it's a road.

12.
What you focus on
is what you tell the universe
you want more of.

13.
Attention is prayer—
you are always
in devotion
to something.

14.
Worry is imagination
held hostage
by fear.

15.
What if you gave
the same focus to joy
as you did to "what if"?

16.
Your dreams bloom
in the sunlight
of sustained vision.

17.
If it hurts—
ask yourself,
"Have I been staring too long
at what is broken?"

18.
Energy flows
toward the question
you keep asking.

19.
Be careful
what you fear.
It may think
you're calling its name.

20.

The soul doesn't chase—
it points.
And creation responds
to where it's looking.

The Law of Flow

The universe is dynamic — always moving, shifting, evolving. Holding on to clutter (physical, emotional, or mental) blocks this natural rhythm. When you let go, new energy flows in. This law is about surrender, releasing the old, and honoring the cycles of creation and clearing.

Key concepts:

- Go with the flow.
- Life is constant movement; holding onto clutter (emotional or physical) blocks blessings.
- Letting go allows new opportunities and relationships to enter.
- Flow requires trust, minimal resistance, and following inner guidance.

THE LAW OF FLOW

"Let go, or be impeded. Life moves where space is made."

1.
Nothing enters a cup
already full—
especially if it's full
of yesterday.

2.
To hoard
is to tell the universe:
"I trust nothing new will come."

3.
What you release,
returns in better form.
What you grip,
grows stale.

4.
Life is a river.
Surrender,
or drown in stillness.

5.
Old thoughts,
like old clothes,
must be shed
to fit who you are becoming.

6.
Even joy decays
when locked in a box.

7.
Let the past
find its place
in the compost.
It was never meant
to be framed.

8.
Clear a drawer,
and watch a decision appear.
Space outside
clears fog inside.

9.
Do not ask for miracles
while clutching dead weight.

10.
Grudges take up
sacred space.
Make room—
and the light will return.

11.
Movement isn't chaos—
it's wisdom
shifting its shape.

12.
Clutter is a prayer
for stuckness.
Decluttering is prophecy.

13.
If nothing new arrives,
look for what refuses
to be released.

14.
Even the earth
lets go of leaves.
Why not you?

15.
Don't just release—
replace.
Let what comes in
match your intention.

16.
You are a vessel.
Not a vault.

17.
Sometimes,
clearing a corner
invites a calling.

18.
Flow is the divine dance
between emptiness
and enough.

19.
Honor the inner tides—
rest, move, breathe,
shed, begin again.

20.
The universe is always flowing.
The only question is:
Are you?

The Law of Abundance

Abundance is not about what you have — it's about what you're open to receive. Love, joy, success, and prosperity are always flowing, but beliefs around unworthiness or fear of lack build walls. This law teaches that to receive more, you must feel worthy of more — and allow it in with gratitude and grace.

Key concepts:

- Abundance is not just material — it includes love, joy, health, and generosity.
- Your beliefs about worthiness directly affect what you allow yourself to receive.
- Abundance flows when you give and receive freely, without blockages.

THE LAW OF ABUNDANCE

"You were never meant to earn the sun. Only to open to it."

1.

Abundance is not earned.
It is allowed.
It arrives through open hearts,
not tightened fists.

2.

To feel rich,
begin with breath.
Then bless the stillness
that asked for nothing.

3.

Abundance waits
at the door of worthiness.
Not the worthiness of doing—
but of being.

4.

The universe is not withholding.
It is waiting
for you to say,
"I am ready to receive."

5.
What you envy in others
points to the part of you
still afraid
you deserve less.

6.
Gratitude
is the doorbell
to abundance.

7.
Scarcity is not real—
it is a belief
repeated into form.

8.
The more you receive,
the more you overflow.
The more you overflow,
the more rivers find you.

9.
Wanting is not the same
as inviting.
You must create the space.

10.
Abundance does not come
because you chase it—

it comes because you've stopped
running from yourself.

11.
Love blocked
is abundance refused.

12.
True abundance is not a mansion—
but a heart
without locks.

13.
A flower blooms
because it trusts
the sun will return.

14.
Do not look for abundance
in the bank alone—
it lives in your laughter,
your rest,
your willingness to be full.

15.
Scarcity clings.
Abundance flows.
One survives.
The other sings.

16.
You cannot keep abundance—
you can only keep allowing it.

17.
When you stop begging life,
it starts giving freely.

18.
Nothing flows toward the one
who insists
they are a drought.

19.
The most abundant soul
is not the one who gathers,
but the one who glows.

20.
Abundance is not found.
It is remembered.
It is what you were
before you were taught
to fear lack.

The Law of Clarity

Confusion clouds manifestation. Clarity sharpens intention and opens new doors. This law reminds us that indecision is also a choice — one that keeps us stuck. Clarity comes from inner alignment, courage to choose, and the willingness to declare what you truly desire.

Key concepts:

- When you are clear, the universe aligns to support you.
- Confusion blocks manifestation; decisions "cut off" noise and open new paths.
- Speak your needs clearly to the universe and trust the response.

THE LAW OF CLARITY

"You cannot receive what you refuse to name."

1.
The fog doesn't lift
until you say
where you are going.

2.
Vague wishes
build vague lives.
Clarity sharpens the blade
of creation.

3.
What you can't name
can't arrive.
The universe delivers
to precise addresses.

4.
To be unclear
is not confusion—
it's a fear
of making a cut.

5.
A decision
is a prayer
spoken with your feet.

6.
Clarity is love
for the future self.
It hands them a map.

7.
When you don't choose,
you still choose—
and usually not well.

8.
The universe cannot answer
a question
you haven't asked properly.

9.
Clarity opens doors
that hesitation
didn't even see.

10.
Confusion thrives
where self-trust
has been silenced.

11.
You cannot be
everything at once.
Let who you *aren't*
fall away.

12.
When you name the dream,
the path begins forming
beneath your feet.

13.
Clarity doesn't rush—
it roots.
It clears the noise
so truth can echo.

14.
A choice made
is a thousand choices silenced.
That is its power.

15.
Do not fear being wrong.
Fear staying vague
for a lifetime.

16.
Even the stars
don't blink
when you finally decide.

17.
Let your "yes" be full.
Let your "no" be kind.
Everything else
is fog.

18.

When you are clear,
others stop
projecting their doubts
onto your silence.

19.

Indecision is exhausting—
clarity is rest.

20.

Your future is not uncertain.
Only your vision of it is.

The Law of Intention

Intention is more than desire — it is directed energy. It aligns you with your purpose and calls the universe to conspire with you. Intention rooted in the highest good creates powerful results, even if the form changes. This law reminds you: the purity of your intent determines the potency of your creation.

Key concepts:

- Intention is more powerful than hope or want — it channels energy toward a goal.
- Karma responds to your intention, not just the outcome.
- Pure intentions for the highest good are always supported.

THE LAW OF INTENTION

"Desire asks. Intention directs."

1.
A wish floats.
An intention walks.
One drifts,
the other delivers.

2.
Intention is alignment
with the river's source—
not shouting at the current,
but moving as one.

3.
When the aim is clear
and clean,
the universe becomes
a bowstring.

4.
You cannot plant seeds
from the ego
and expect heaven's harvest.

5.
What matters is not
what you want—
but why.

6.
The law reads your motives
like fingerprints.
Nothing pure
goes unseen.

7.
Even if it fails,
a noble intention
succeeds in spirit.

8.
Intent carves the tunnel
through which reality flows.

9.
If your energy is scattered,
so will be the result.

10.
To intend
is to announce your arrival
before the door exists.

11.
You can say a thousand words—
but the universe listens
to where your arrow is aimed.

12.
Set an intention,
not to *get*,
but to *become*.

13.
An intention born from fear
becomes an anchor.
One born from truth
becomes a sail.

14.
The smallest action
done with sacred intent
outweighs grand gestures
hollow with noise.

15.
Do not just visualize.
Set your inner compass
by the light behind it.

16.
The clearer your "why,"
the less your "how"
needs to struggle.

17.

What you intend
shapes the path—
even if it's slow,
it bends that way.

18.

Intention is the sacred contract
you sign
before reality fulfills it.

19.

Let the intention rise
from the soul,
not the scarcity.

20.

When the energy behind the act
is clean,
the outcome cannot miss you.

The Law of Prosperity

Prosperity begins with your mindset. Fear, hoarding, or guilt around money creates energetic blocks. Generosity and self-worth unlock flow. Prosperity is about allowing yourself to feel supported, nourished, and expansive — in all areas of life.

Key concepts:

- Prosperity is a mindset. Fear, hoarding, and unworthiness block it.
- Generosity and wise use of resources attract prosperity.
- Speak, act, and live as though you are already prosperous.

THE LAW OF PROSPERITY

"What you believe you're worth, you make space to receive."

1.
Prosperity begins
where fear of not having
ends.

2.
It's not about gold.
It's about flow.
It's not about more.
It's about ease.

3.
You will never attract wealth
by worshiping lack.

4.
The miser and the beggar
both believe
in poverty.

5.
Your wallet
echoes your thoughts.
So does your joy.

6.
To feel prosperous,
give.
To stay prosperous,
receive.

7.
Greed is not love of wealth—
it is fear in disguise.

8.
Prosperity has nothing to do
with how much you own—
but how open you are.

9.
Tight fists
make terrible magnets.

10.
You do not have to earn
your right to thrive—
only remember it.

11.
To hoard is to say:
"I do not trust
life to provide again."

12.
Prosperity visits
where energy is generous.

13.
Rigid minds
create rigid lives.
Prosperity needs movement,
not walls.

14.
The richer the soil,
the easier the seed.
What is your inner earth like?

15.
Every time you say,
"I'm not good enough,"
you slam the door
on grace.

16.
Abundance is a song.
Prosperity is knowing
you're allowed to sing it.

17.
You were born worthy.
The rest is forgetting.

18.
Prosperity is not a goal—
it's a state
that matches your beliefs.

19.
Look at how you spend.
You're always teaching the universe
what to send.

20.
Speak to money
as you would to a friend:
with trust,
with joy,
with welcome.

The Law of Manifestation

You are always manifesting. The question is: are you doing it consciously? Manifestation combines thought, feeling, belief, clarity, and vibration. The key is alignment. If you vibrate in lack but visualize abundance, the lack will win. This law teaches precision, presence, and unwavering faith.

Key concepts:

- Look around. You've manifested everything in your life through vibration, thoughts, and beliefs.
- Clarity, faith, visualization, and alignment are key steps.
- Be what you seek to attract; manifestation is vibrational, not mental alone.
- "What you seek, is seeking you" - *Rumi*

THE LAW OF MANIFESTATION

"You manifest what you match — not what you want."

1.

Manifestation is not magic—
it is alignment.
You tune yourself
and reality echoes.

2.

You've manifested everything—
even the parts you pretend
you didn't ask for.

3.

A foggy vision
creates a foggy form.
Be clear—
or be surprised.

4.

Desire lights the flame.
Clarity sharpens it.
Faith sustains the burn.

5.

You don't get what you imagine—
you get what you vibrate.

6.
The image must live in you
without resistance
before it can walk beside you.

7.
Manifestation listens
to the emotion,
not the sentence.

8.
To manifest love,
you must love being
the one who gives it.

9.
When you align fully,
the path builds itself.

10.
Write it, name it,
feel it, see it.
Then become it—
and let go.

11.
If doubt walks with you,
what you call
will lose its way.

12.
Faith is not a mood.
It is your side of the contract.

13.
Before it exists out there,
it must exist
without trembling
in you.

14.
If your wish is dressed
in fear,
the universe will pause.

15.
What you *almost* believe
stays just out of reach.

16.
To manifest
is not to control—
it is to co-create
with the unseen.

17.
Picture it.
Then match it.
Then act as if
it's already knocking.

18.

Some things manifest slowly
not because they are far,
but because you still
doubt your worth.

19.

The clearer the picture,
the quicker the arrival.
Clarity opens the gate.

20.

Manifestation begins
not when you speak—
but when your body
believes the words.

The Law of Success

Success is alignment — between your vibration and your vision. It's not achieved through struggle, but through clarity, self-belief, and consistent energetic harmony. This law reminds you: what you believe is possible determines what becomes real.

Key concepts:

- Success is energy alignment, not luck or struggle.
- Clear vision, self-belief, and vibrational resonance create success.
- Letting go and flowing with purpose activates this law.

THE LAW OF SUCCESS

"Success is not a destination — it's a resonance."

1.

Success arrives
when your belief
no longer contradicts
your vision.

2.

It's not how hard you work—
it's how aligned you are
as you move.

3.

Success does not bloom
from force.
It blooms
where flow is honored.

4.

A cluttered mind
cannot hold a clear result.

5.

You must see yourself
already standing there
before the path
appears beneath your feet.

6.
Success whispers—
but fear shouts.
Which voice
have you trained yourself to follow?

7.
You don't chase success.
You tune yourself
until it recognizes you.

8.
The outer win
follows the inner shift.
Always.

9.
Believe in your worth,
and doors appear
where there were only walls.

10.
Success is self-trust
written into reality.

11.
The soul's success
is not in applause,
but in peace.

12.
Align.
Believe.
Release.
That is the quiet formula
no one teaches.

13.
Let go of the outcome.
Hold fast to the frequency.

14.
If you fear success,
you'll slow it down
by accident.

15.
Your energy precedes your name.
Let it speak
of fulfillment.

16.
You do not arrive at success—
you remember
that it was always yours.

17.
Celebrate each step.
Joy is part of the code.

18.

Be what you seek,
and it will seek you.

19.

Nothing succeeds like sincerity.
The universe does not support
a mask.

20.

Success is not luck—
it's law.
And law responds
to truth.

Part III – The Laws of Higher Awareness

Awakening the soul through integration, responsibility, and inner mastery.

This set of laws shifts your path from creation to conscious evolution. These are the principles of karma, reincarnation, polarity, and discernment—laws that govern your growth across lifetimes. They ask you to see the bigger picture: how challenges serve your soul, how every act sows karmic seeds, and how you carry spiritual contracts beyond a single life.

Here, awareness replaces reaction. By taking radical responsibility for your beliefs, affirmations, emotions, and choices, you become an active participant in your soul's evolution. The laws of prayer, meditation, and challenge help you align with higher truths and navigate Earth's duality with strength and grace.

LAWS OF HIGHER AWARENESS

Where the seeker becomes the witness, and the witness becomes the light.

1.

This is the path
beyond wanting—
where life becomes
lesson,
and every challenge
a disguised friend.

2.

Higher awareness does not avoid pain—
it names it, meets it,
transforms it.

3.

You are not here
to escape the world,
but to see through it.

4.

Every law beyond this point
is not about gaining—
but remembering
who you were
before forgetting began.

5.

The soul does not grow
in comfort.
It grows in clarity.
It grows when you ask,
"What is this really teaching me?"

The Law of Balance and Polarity

Life moves in opposites. Joy and sorrow, power and vulnerability, action and rest — all are part of wholeness. Your soul seeks balance through experiencing polarity. It invites you to honor both sides of every experience — not to judge one as better, but to integrate them both. Every soul evolves by encountering contrast — light and dark, power and surrender, joy and pain. This law teaches that all extremes are divine tools for awakening. Instead of resisting one side, you are asked to find stillness in the center. Harmony is achieved not by avoidance, but by integration.

Key concepts:

- The soul evolves by experiencing opposites (rich/poor, male/female, etc.).
- True growth happens by integrating and balancing polarities within.
- Aim for wholeness and inner neutrality.

THE LAW OF BALANCE & POLARITY

"To know peace, one must walk through both fire and water."

1.
You must know silence
to hear the song.
You must know shadow
to greet your light.

2.
The universe is made of two hands:
one gives,
one receives.
Both are yours.

3.
Darkness is not evil—
it is instruction.
Without it,
you'd never understand
the radiance you hold.

4.
The soul does not choose sides.
It seeks center.

5.
Every extreme
invites its opposite—

not as punishment,
but as return.

6.
You were once the oppressor.
You will be the healer too.
This is how the soul rounds its edge.

7.
Pain does not cancel joy.
It teaches you
how deeply joy can live.

8.
Balance is not sameness—
it is sacred tension
held in grace.

9.
When you cling too tightly
to one side,
life lovingly
pulls you back.

10.
Each polarity is a doorway.
Walk through enough of them—
and you stop fearing the next one.

11.
To only know light
is to be half-blind.

12.
Masculine and feminine
are not war,
but weaving.

13.
The soul reincarnates
to taste the full circle—
weak and strong,
silent and seen.

14.
Wealth without wisdom
requires a life of poverty
to understand what richness is.

15.
Do not curse your imbalance.
It is the force
that leads you home.

16.
Even peace, when clung to,
becomes stagnation.

17.

You do not grow
by avoiding your shadows.
You grow
by integrating them.

18.

Every swing of the pendulum
makes you more whole.

19.

You are both seed and sky.
The trick is remembering
when to root
and when to rise.

20.

Polarity is not conflict—
it is contrast.
And contrast
is how the Divine paints.

The Law of Karma

Karma is a sacred echo — every thought, word, and action returns to you in perfect timing and form. Karma is the spiritual law of cause and effect. Every action, thought, and emotion sows a seed. What you give returns — in form, in timing, in energy. Karma is not punishment, but a precise balancing mechanism. The key is awareness: live intentionally, and your return becomes a blessing.

Key concepts:

- Karma is cause and effect; every thought, word, and deed creates ripples.
- Your family, health, and life circumstances are karmically chosen.
- High-vibration souls receive instant karma; kindness and love create credits.

THE LAW OF KARMA

"You do not escape your energy — you inherit it."

1.

Every thought you plant
ripens—
in this life
or the next.

2.

Karma is not revenge—
it is return.
The echo
of your own becoming.

3.

You cannot run from it—
because you are it.
Karma walks beside you
as your shadow's shadow.

4.

It keeps no score,
only balance.
It does not punish—
it teaches.

5.

Your kindness today
may bloom
in a stranger's smile
years from now.

6.

That parent,
that partner,
that child—
they are soul mirrors
from other lifetimes,
here to finish the sentence.

7.

Karma is not bound
by clocks.
It waits
until you're listening.

8.

Sometimes karma is harsh
only because
you haven't yet
softened into awareness.

9.

You were not born into this life
by mistake.
You chose it—
lesson, bloodline, body, name.

10.
If you never get away with anything,
it means
you're evolving.

11.
Your health is karma.
So is your voice.
So is your silence.

12.
To love again
those who once hurt you—
this is grace
rewriting your karma.

13.
Whatever you give
with intention,
returns
when you've forgotten.

14.
The more conscious you become,
the quicker the return.
Instant karma
is a mark
of spiritual readiness.

15.
No one gets away—
but everyone gets a chance
to give back.

16.
Mindsets are inherited karma.
Beliefs shape lifetimes.

17.
Forgive yourself—
not to escape karma,
but to meet it
with compassion.

18.
To heal another
is to repay a forgotten debt
with light.

19.
Karma is neither cruel
nor kind.
It is precise.
It is just.

20.

Plant goodness
not for this life alone—
but for the thousand
yet to come.

The Law of Reincarnation

The soul is eternal. It returns to Earth repeatedly to resolve, grow, heal, and evolve. Patterns you face in this life often have roots in another. You chose your family, your lessons, and your body — all to support your soul's expansion, heal karmic bonds, and expand in light. Every relationship, struggle, and gift has been chosen before birth with purpose. This law invites compassion for the deeper story. It encourages you to see beyond this life, and to treat your path as a chapter in your soul's long story.

Key concepts:

- You return to resolve unfinished lessons, heal past harms, and expand spiritually.
- Souls reincarnate in families and communities to evolve through recurring patterns.
- Earth is a school; each life is a classroom.

THE LAW OF REINCARNATION

"You return not as punishment — but to remember what you forgot."

1.
You have worn
a thousand names.
And each time,
you only ever sought
to remember one:
your own.

2.
Reincarnation is not repetition—
it is refinement.

3.
You return
because some stories
weren't finished—
and some wounds
refused to close.

4.
The soul takes its time.
It returns not to escape karma,
but to complete
what love began.

5.

Sometimes your child
was once your mother.
Sometimes your enemy
was once your healer.

6.

You come back
to feel it all—
from both sides.

7.

The soul is not linear.
It spirals—
ascending,
unfolding,
returning only
to rise again.

8.

No lifetime is wasted.
Even in forgetting,
the soul learns
to wake.

9.

You may not remember,
but your bones do.
Your fears, your gifts—

all carry
ancient fingerprints.

10.
This is not your first heartbreak.
Nor your first miracle.
You are older
than your name.

11.
A soul returns
not for pleasure,
but for precision.
Each life
a refinement of light.

12.
Sometimes,
you are sent back
not for yourself—
but for someone
you once broke.

13.
Karma doesn't forget.
But it does forgive—
once you've truly lived
the other side.

14.
Even the pause
between lives
teaches.

15.
You chose your family.
Yes—
even the difficult ones.

16.
Earth is a school
with no grades—
only lessons
you must feel.

17.
You are not starting over—
you are continuing
an invisible symphony.

18.
Each soul you meet
has met you before.
This is not a beginning—
just another meeting.

19.
When you stop judging others,
you begin to understand
your past lives.

20.
You will return,
not because you failed,
but because
you still have love to give.

The Law of Responsibility

Responsibility means ownership — not for others, but for your vibration, choices, and path. You are responsible for your energy, your choices, your healing. Blame and projection disempower you. Responsibility is not burden — it's liberation. It is the bridge between victimhood and empowerment. When you own your life, you reclaim your power. This law calls you into sovereignty. It reminds you that your reactions shape your future more than your conditions do. Freedom begins the moment you stop blaming and start responding.

Key concepts:

- Responsibility is the ability to respond appropriately.
- You are accountable for your emotions, reactions, choices, and destiny.
- Taking on others' karma or emotional burdens disempowers them.

THE LAW OF RESPONSIBILITY

"Everything in your life reflects your ability to respond — not to blame."

1.
Nothing changes
until you own it.
Nothing heals
until you claim your part.

2.
Responsibility
is not a burden—
it's the key
to your freedom.

3.
Blame is easy.
But growth
never grows
in someone else's soil.

4.
Every choice,
every silence,
every look away—
was a direction
you gave the universe.

5.

You are not at fault
for what broke you—
but you are responsible
for what you build next.

6.

Your home,
your body,
your energy—
they respond to how you treat them.
And they speak on your behalf.

7.

To carry what is yours
is power.
To carry what isn't—
is karma.

8.

You were never meant
to fix everyone.
You were meant
to live as an example
of healed self.

9.

Even your sadness
asks:
"What will you do with me?"

10.
If the same story repeats,
check the role
you keep signing up for.

11.
Taking responsibility
is choosing
to become the cause
of your joy.

12.
Don't save them.
Strengthen them.
That's love.

13.
You cannot walk their path—
but you can stand
as a lighthouse
while they choose their own way.

14.
Every gift you neglect
becomes a burden.

15.

Responsibility doesn't mean
doing it alone.
It means not expecting
someone else
to do it *for* you.

16.

To respond instead of react
is a mark
of mastery.

17.

If you can't say it
because they'll get angry—
you're carrying
their feelings
on your back.

18.

Even your silence
has a signature.
Make sure it speaks truth.

19.

Responsibility is the bridge
between who you are
and who you're becoming.

20.

You can't rewrite the past—
but you can answer it
with integrity.

The Law of Discrimination / Discernment

Discernment is the art of spiritual intelligence — knowing what is aligned and what is illusion. Not every voice within, is your higher self; Not all guidance is true. Not all intuition is clear. This law reminds you to test the energy behind people, ideas, and experiences. Discernment is not judgment — it is wisdom born of intuition and self-trust. Your inner compass must be consulted often. It urges you to sharpen your intuition, question energies, and feel before following. Discernment protects your soul and purifies your choices.

Key concepts:

- Intuition (gut feeling) is your inner compass.
- Discernment is necessary to distinguish truth from illusion.
- Failure to discern creates karmic consequences.

THE LAW OF DISCRIMINATION

(also known as The Law of Discernment)
"Not everything you feel is yours. Not everything you hear is true."

1.
Your soul speaks softly.
Discernment
is learning to turn down the world
until you hear it.

2.
Not every light
leads home.
Even gold
can distract the seeker.

3.
Discernment is not judgment—
it is clarity
with compassion.

4.
If the voice speaks through fear,
it is not your highest self.

5.
The more light you carry,
the more shadows test you.
Not all warmth
is fire.

6.
To discern
is to pause long enough
to feel what *feels like truth.*

7.
You are allowed
to say no
to what sparkles
but does not serve.

8.
Even angels
are questioned by those
who walk awake.

9.
Check the energy—
not the words.

10.
Discernment sharpens
as the soul deepens.
It grows in silence,
not in noise.

11.

Your body always knows.
Your mind may argue—
but your gut
never lies.

12.

You do not owe your trust
to every smile.
Trust is sacred currency.

13.

Discernment is a muscle—
built through choice,
strengthened through stillness.

14.

Even beauty
can seduce.
Even peace
can be false.

15.

Ask:
Does this contract my heart,
or expand it?

16.

Discernment doesn't always explain—
but it always knows.

17.

You don't need proof.
You need permission
to trust what you already feel.

18.

There are many paths—
but only one
will hum with your name.

19.

If it drains you,
if it dims you,
if it dulls your joy—
it is not meant
to walk with you.

20.

The wise do not fear illusion.
They simply
see through it.

The Law of Affirmation

What you affirm becomes your truth. Every word you repeat becomes a pattern your subconscious starts to believe. Your subconscious mind receives every repeated word and image as instruction. This law teaches that *spoken thought carries creative power*. Affirmations are tools to reprogram belief and raise vibration. Positive affirmations rewire your energy field, replacing doubt with divine identity. When declared with conviction, they reshape your inner and outer reality. Speak in the now, with love, and with certainty.

Key concepts:

- Repetition of thoughts (positive or negative) programs your subconscious.
- Affirm in the present tense with emotional energy.
- The universe reflects your beliefs back to you.

THE LAW OF AFFIRMATION

"What you repeat becomes real. What you believe becomes you."

1.
Your words are architects.
Each sentence
lays the bones
of your becoming.

2.
Every time you say
"I am…"
you cast a spell
on your reality.

3.
The universe doesn't hear
whether it's true yet.
It hears how often
you say it.

4.
You are not lying
when you affirm—
you are choosing
a new truth
to become real.

5.
Affirmation isn't magic—
it's training the soul
to believe again.

6.
The unconscious mind
does not filter.
It receives each word
like law.

7.
Speak with care.
Your cells are listening.
Your life is listening.

8.
Say:
"I am worthy."
"I am light."
"I am ready."
And then notice
how life starts rearranging.

9.
If you always say,
"Nothing ever works out,"
the universe replies,
"As you wish."

10.
Affirm not to convince—
but to remember.

11.
Even if you whisper,
your soul will hear.
Say only what you want
to grow.

12.
The more energy you place
behind a thought,
the deeper it roots.

13.
A simple phrase
spoken with belief
is more powerful
than a thousand wishes.

14.
Let your affirmations
be now.
"I will be"
never arrives.

15.
If you cannot speak it yet,
write it.

Ink is prayer
with patience.

16.
Your inner world
becomes your address.
Affirmation is your change of residence.

17.
Negative affirmations
are still affirmations.
Be careful
what you claim.

18.
What you affirm
does not only shape you—
it calls new mirrors into your life.

19.
Say it until the voice inside
stops laughing.
Then say it louder.

20.
Affirmation is not pretending.
It is prophesying
with love.

The Law of Prayer

Prayer is conscious connection — a bridge between the seen and unseen. Prayer is not just a request it's alignment with divine intelligence. When asked with trust and clarity, the universe listens and responds through timing, symbols, and guidance.

Every thought is a prayer. Worry is a prayer for what you don't want. This law invites you to pray with belief, faith, surrender, and receptivity — trusting that the universe always answers. It teaches that prayer is received not by words alone, but by the vibration behind them. To pray is to collaborate with Source.

Key concepts:

- All thoughts are prayers; worry is a negative prayer.
- Ask with faith, release attachment, and prepare to receive.
- Prayer aligns your vibration with divine will.

THE LAW OF PRAYER

"Every thought is a prayer. The question is: what are you praying for?"

1.

You are always praying—
with your words,
your worries,
your whispers.

2.

Worry is a prayer
for what you don't want.
So be mindful
where your fear kneels.

3.

A true prayer
is not begging—
it is aligning.

4.

The moment you ask,
start preparing
to receive.

5.

The universe responds
not to desperation,
but to devotion.

6.
Say it once.
Then let your faith
do the repeating.

7.
Prayer does not change God.
It changes the one
who dares to ask.

8.
When you pray,
don't just speak.
Feel it.
See it.
Let it live inside you.

9.
Silence can be prayer.
So can breath.
So can tears.

10.
Thank the unseen
as though it's already here—
and soon it will be.

11.
A powerful prayer
carries no tension.
Only trust.

12.
You don't need perfect words.
You need an honest heart.

13.
Pray for the highest good—
not for control.
The divine sees farther than you do.

14.
Don't rush it.
Prayer ripens
like fruit in the sun.

15.
Every "why"
can become a "thank you"
with time.

16.
Prayer without faith
is just noise.

17.
Pray not only
for outcomes,
but for insight.

18.
Some prayers arrive
disguised as people.
Some as pauses.

19.
Even your longing
is sacred.
Let it rise
like smoke.

20.
You are not asking
from below.
You are remembering
your right to speak
with the stars.

The Law of Meditation

Meditation quiets the mind so the soul can speak. It quiets the noise so you can hear the truth. It dissolves resistance and brings your awareness back to center. It is the doorway to your inner sanctuary, where truth, clarity, and divine presence reside. This law reveals that silence is not empty — it is rich with instruction. Meditation strengthens your light body, sharpens awareness, and restores balance. It is about returning to the presence where guidance and peace live.

Key concepts:

- Meditation silences mental chatter and opens channels for divine wisdom.
- Stillness restores balance and connects you with the true Self.
- Practiced regularly, it supports healing, insight, and soul alignment.

THE LAW OF MEDITATION

"Stillness is not escape — it is return."

1.

Meditation is not silence—
it is listening.

2.

You are not your thoughts.
You are the sky
they float across.

3.

Stillness doesn't come
when the mind is empty—
but when the soul is heard.

4.

Every breath
is an invitation
to come home.

5.

In the space between thoughts
lives a gate—
walk through it.

6.
You are not trying
to feel nothing.
You are trying
to feel everything
without drowning.

7.
The monkey mind
climbs less
when it knows
you're watching.

8.
Meditation isn't about doing.
It's about being done.

9.
The deeper you go,
the less you need.
Even desire
softens in the light.

10.
A single moment
of true presence
can reroute a lifetime.

11.

Sit not to empty—
but to align.

12.

Inhale.
Not to fill—
but to receive.
Exhale.
Not to lose—
but to return.

13.

You've been looking
everywhere.
Now look within.

14.

Meditation is not absence.
It is arrival.

15.

No posture is perfect
without surrender.

16.

The soul speaks softly.
Meditation turns up the volume.

17.

Do not fight the thoughts.
Watch them pass—
like weather over a mountain.

18.

Stillness is not a state—
it's a frequency.
And you can tune to it
anywhere.

19.

The answers you seek
are beneath
your third breath.

20.

You don't meditate
to escape the world.
You meditate
to move through it
as light.

The Law of Challenge

Challenge is not a block — it is a gate. Every test is placed in your path to strengthen your discernment, refine your light, and prepare you for greater alignment. Challenge is your soul's filter. It helps you test energy, and protect your path. This law teaches you to question, to pause, and to respond from clarity. Don't accept everything at face value. Ask questions. Check intentions. Strengthen your light until nothing false can deceive you. True spiritual maturity is measured by how you meet resistance.

Key concepts:

- You must question, test, and discern energies, beings, and situations.
- Challenges reveal spiritual strength and protect your path.
- Light grows stronger through conscious response to darkness.

THE LAW OF CHALLENGE

"You are not punished by challenges — you are prepared through them."

1.

Every challenge
is a disguised doorway—
the test is whether
you try to run
or walk through.

2.

The universe doesn't ask,
"Are you comfortable?"
It asks,
"Are you ready to rise?"

3.

Difficulty is the soul's weightlifting.
Without resistance,
you stay soft.

4.

Don't curse the fire.
It's turning you
into something
that won't burn.

5.
A challenge only hurts
until you understand
what it came to teach.

6.
Sometimes it's not a punishment—
it's a promotion in disguise.

7.
If it pushes your buttons,
it's because it came
to unplug them.

8.
Every mountain
is an invitation
to grow new legs.

9.
You don't get to skip
what will shape you.

10.
The soul contracts for pressure
so the light within
can expand.

11.
Even betrayal
has a purpose—
it peels away
what was not yours.

12.
To question is holy.
To challenge the illusion
is an act of awakening.

13.
You are allowed to doubt—
just don't forget to listen
afterward.

14.
That storm you survived?
It was carving out space
for your next miracle.

15.
A spiritual warrior isn't fearless.
They just bow to the challenge
instead of running from it.

16.
When everything falls apart,
look for what remained.
That's what was real.

17.
Even your delays
are teachers.

18.
The test doesn't end
when the world changes—
but when you do.

19.
Challenge is the universe's way
of showing you
your own strength.

20.
You asked for growth.
So it gave you
a mirror that cracked
until you looked in.

Part IV – The Laws of Higher Frequency

Living as light — transmuting reality through energy, love, and presence.

This final set of laws guides you into subtle realms of vibration, grace, and oneness. They teach that frequency is your true identity—and that when you raise your vibration, you unlock the miraculous. Gratitude, blessings, decrees, and faith all operate at frequencies that transcend karma and allow you to create through alignment, not effort.

Purification, healing, and forgiveness dissolve the density that keeps you bound. As you become clearer, lighter, and more loving, the universe responds in kind. The Law of One reminds you that all is connected—and that every act of love you extend ripples across creation.

LAWS OF HIGHER FREQUENCY

A realm beyond resistance — where light leads, and being becomes blessing.

1.

You are entering the space
where matter bends to spirit—
where stillness heals
and presence transforms.

2.

Here, the laws are not forced—
they are felt.
They respond to your purity,
not your pressure.

3.

This is where vibration speaks louder than words.
Where grace, faith, and light
carry more weight
than action.

4.

No longer about doing.
Only about aligning.
Only about remembering
you already are
what you seek.

5.

The more love you hold,
the less you need.
The higher you rise,
the gentler the steps.

The Law of Frequency / Vibration

Everything in existence vibrates — your thoughts, your body, your words, your emotions. Everything is energy. Your feelings emit a frequency. Low vibrations attract heaviness; high vibrations attract grace. This law reveals that your frequency determines what you experience and attract. It teaches mastery of energy through self-awareness. To raise your life, raise your vibration through love, clarity, service, and joy. What you are energetically is what you live and experience.

Key concepts:

- Emotions and thoughts carry vibrations; love is high, fear is low.
- Like attracts like — your vibration determines your experiences.
- Raise vibration through joy, service, love, and authenticity.

THE LAW OF FREQUENCY / VIBRATION

"You do not attract what you say. You attract what you are."

1.

Your words may whisper love—
but your frequency
always tells the truth.

2.

You are a tuning fork.
Each moment
you strike your own chord—
and the world responds
in harmony.

3.

Vibration is your true identity.
Before your name,
before your face,
you were a frequency.

4.

Low thoughts
darken your light.
But joy—
joy shines like a bell
heard through dimensions.

5.
Anger is not evil.
But hold it too long—
and it lowers
what you came here to lift.

6.
What you do from love
is high-frequency.
What you do from guilt
is heavy to carry.

7.
Your presence walks
into a room
before your feet do.

8.
The energy you carry
is more honest
than any introduction.

9.
To change your life,
don't fight it.
Change your frequency.

10.

You cannot fake light.
It either radiates,
or it doesn't.

11.

The body feels it.
The animals sense it.
Only the mind
doubts it.

12.

Shame is a low sound.
Gratitude
sings a higher note.

13.

Every habit
either tunes you up
or tunes you out.

14.

What you consume
becomes your vibration.
What you dwell on
becomes your code.

15.

Let your kindness rise
not for approval—

but because it's who you are
when fear falls silent.

16.
Low frequency
feels like effort.
High frequency
feels like flow.

17.
You are not stuck—
you are just resonating
at an old version of you.

18.
Even your silence
has a vibration.
Make it sacred.

19.
Raise your frequency—
and watch what no longer fits
fall away without a fight.

20.
You do not need to scream
to be heard
in the language of light.

The Law of Miracles

Miracles bypass the rules of density. Miracles happen when your energy becomes clear and aligned with divine flow. They are not random — they are the result of high-frequency consciousness overriding karmic resistance and dissolving limitations. There are no coincidences, only synchronicities. This law teaches that miracles are normal at elevated states. When your heart is open and your belief is pure, the impossible unfolds.

Key concepts:

- Miracles occur when divine frequency overrides karmic density.
- Forgiveness, surrender, and divine alignment enable miracles.
- Ask with purity and be open — miracles are natural at high vibration.

THE LAW OF MIRACLES

"When your vibration rises, the impossible becomes natural."

1.

A miracle is not a break in the rules—
it's what happens
when you rise above them.

2.

Miracles don't arrive by force—
they arrive by frequency.

3.

When you align with love,
life bends
to bless you.

4.

You are never waiting
for the miracle.
It's waiting
for you to become
the version of you
who lets it in.

5.

Forgiveness
is the doorway
miracles prefer to use.

6.
What looks like coincidence
is often just divinity
with its mask on.

7.
Ask.
Align.
Let go.
That is the quiet ritual
behind every wonder.

8.
You don't have to earn them—
you only have to stop resisting
what is already trying
to find you.

9.
Miracles are natural.
Doubt is what feels unnatural
to the soul.

10.
The higher your vibration,
the shorter the distance
between desire and reality.

11.
Even your tears
can become holy water
when love flows through them.

12.
If the miracle delays,
it's because you're still growing
into the self
who can hold it.

13.
They don't always look
how you imagined.
But they always feel
like home.

14.
Sometimes the miracle
is not the healing—
but the transformation
that came through the wound.

15.
Miracles are timed
to the soul's awakening—
not the mind's impatience.

16.
You don't manifest a miracle—
you become a match for one.

17.
Gratitude
opens the gate.
Grace
walks through it.

18.
You've already lived
a thousand miracles.
You just called them
something else.

19.
They arrive
when you're present—
not perfect.

20.
A miracle is simply
divine order
revealing itself.

The Law of Healing

Healing occurs when stagnant energy is released and replaced with light. Healing is the restoration of wholeness across body, mind, and soul. Illness often results from unresolved or suppressed emotions, tension, energetic imprints, or karmic blockage. This law reminds you that true healing happens on all levels — physical, emotional, mental, and spiritual. It involves illumination — bringing light into the dark places. Release, forgiveness, and presence are your medicine.

Key concepts:

- Illness results from stagnant or suppressed energy.
- Healing restores flow and often requires emotional or karmic release.
- Divine healing must be requested and honored by the soul's path.

THE LAW OF HEALING

"When light enters what was hidden, wholeness begins."

1.

Healing doesn't mean
you were broken—
it means a part of you
is returning
home.

2.

Disease begins
where energy stops moving.
Let it move—
and life flows back in.

3.

The body never lies.
It stores the stories
your voice couldn't tell.

4.

Healing starts
the moment you stop
fighting what wants
to be seen.

5.
Love moves through
blocked energy
like sunlight
melting frost.

6.
No healing lasts
if guilt is kept
in the basement.

7.
Forgiveness
is not just emotional—
it's cellular.

8.
To heal the body,
speak kindly
to the spirit within it.

9.
Pain is a messenger—
not a punishment.

10.
You must first believe
you are allowed to heal.
Then you will.

11.
Holding anger too long
is like drinking fire
to stay warm.

12.
Healing is rarely instant—
but always sacred.

13.
What you suppress
becomes the signal
your body tries to amplify.

14.
You are not just muscle
and mind—
you are memory, light,
and vibration.

15.
Sometimes the healer
is a stranger.
Sometimes it is
stillness.

16.
Stop asking,
"When will it be gone?"
Ask instead,
"What does it still need me
to feel?"

17.
To be healed
is not to forget—
but to remember
without pain.

18.
You cannot rush
what unfolds
on soul time.

19.
Healing is permission
to be whole
in a world
that profits off your pieces.

20.
True healing happens
when you stop identifying
with the wound.

The Law of Purification

Purity attracts light. The aura, like a magnetic field, must be clear for higher energies to enter. To carry more light, you must release what is dense. This law teaches that cleansing your aura, mind, and surroundings, clears space for divine energy. Emotional heaviness, toxic habits, and spiritual clutter block clarity and protection. Purification invites you to be a clear vessel for higher guidance and love, so your soul can radiate and receive the highest.

Key concepts:

- The aura reflects your energetic state — a clear aura is protection; a murky aura holds unresolved emotions, negativity, addictions.
- Earth, air, fire, and water are purifying forces — walking barefoot, hugging trees, bathing in the rain, sea salt baths, decluttering, bring clarity.
- Negative behaviors and thoughts (swearing, mess, overwork, addiction, resentment, etc.) contaminate the aura Irritability, clutter, fatigue are signs purification is needed.

THE LAW OF PURIFICATION

"To hold more light, you must release what clouds it."

1.

Your aura is your true skin.
When it's clean,
nothing can cling.

2.

You are not being punished—
you are being polished.

3.

Old anger
becomes mold in the soul.
Scrub it with forgiveness.

4.

You cannot ascend
carrying dust.

5.

The clutter on your shelf
is the echo
of clutter in your thoughts.

6.
When you're irritable for no reason,
the reason is residue.

7.
Negative habits
are simply grief
that was never asked
to leave.

8.
To purify
is not to deny—
but to release
with reverence.

9.
Swearing poisons the air.
Gratitude clears it.

10.
Salt doesn't just season—
it sanctifies.
Soak and let it draw
the darkness out.

11.
Burn the letters.
Not to forget—
but to transform.

12.
Walk barefoot on the grass.
Let the Earth
pull your sorrow
back into wisdom.

13.
The body holds
what the voice avoids.
Speak the truth—
and the body will exhale.

14.
Smoke rises
because it's free.
So does the soul
after purification.

15.
Wind cleanses more
than windows.
Let it pass through your mind.

16.
An aura weighed with shame
dims even the most radiant soul.

17.
No angel enters
a room still soaked
in bitterness.

18.
The world, too,
needs clearing.
Speak light into the land.

19.
Darkness is not evil—
just stagnant light.
Set it moving.

20.
To purify
is to prepare
for the divine.

The Law of Perspective

Reality is shaped by perception. Your consciousness determines what you see — and how large or small a problem appears. Your perception *defines* your reality. From a low vibration, problems seem enormous; from higher awareness, they reveal purpose. This law teaches that shifting how you see is often more powerful than changing what is seen. Expanding your perspective dissolves suffering and invites deeper understanding. Wisdom begins when you ask, "What is this trying to teach me?"

Key concepts:

- Time and experience are perceived through vibration and mindset.
- Judgment limits awareness; higher perspective sees all as divine.
- Changing your viewpoint changes your reality.
- Everyone sees reality differently based on their level of awareness.

THE LAW OF PERSPECTIVE

"What you see depends on where you stand — and how wide your eyes are open."

1.
Time moves slowly
only for those
still trapped in fear.

2.
The problem
is not always the thing—
but how close you're standing to it.

3.
A mountain shrinks
when viewed from a mile above.
So does pain.

4.
Perspective is the secret
behind every miracle.
Nothing changed—
but everything felt different.

5.
To a child,
a shadow is a monster.
To the wise,

it's just the sun
in a new position.

6.
Every person lives
in a world of their own making—
do not assume
you've seen theirs.

7.
What feels unbearable today
may tomorrow
be the reason you awaken.

8.
You cannot judge
what you do not understand.
And you rarely understand
what you've not yet lived.

9.
Shift the angle.
What once seemed loss
now reveals itself
as release.

10.
A soul can be noble
even in a beggar's body.

11.
Someone sees cruelty.
Someone sees karma.
Someone sees
a lesson beginning.

12.
Even war
can birth compassion
in the soul brave enough
to look deeper.

13.
You are not wrong—
you are incomplete.
Keep expanding.

14.
Sometimes,
what looks like betrayal
was simply redirection
from the divine.

15.
If they push your buttons,
ask what mirror they're holding up.

16.
You do not need
to agree
to understand.

17.
Judgment says,
"This is wrong."
Perspective asks,
"What don't I yet see?"

18.
Your enemy
is just you
from a different angle.

19.
In the dark,
every shape feels threatening.
Turn on the light
and you'll find
your own coat on the chair.

20.
Perspective doesn't change the truth—
it reveals a larger one.

The Law of Gratitude

Gratitude is a spiritual amplifier. It multiplies blessings. What you thank grows. When you give thanks, even in struggle, you signal abundance — and the universe responds in kind. This law teaches that appreciation multiplies blessings, while complaint dims your light. It is a magnetic force — one that draws in peace, abundance, and happiness. Gratitude is a frequency of trust, joy, and receptivity.

Key concepts:

- Gratitude is a high-frequency generator of abundance.
- Thanking life amplifies its gifts; complaints block them.
- Focus on blessings, even in difficulty, to attract more.
- Challenges carry hidden lessons — gratitude unlocks their purpose.

THE LAW OF GRATITUDE

"What you thank becomes more. Gratitude is the magnet of miracles."

1.

Gratitude isn't payment.
It's permission
for life to flow freely again.

2.

The more you count your blessings,
the more the universe
loses count.

3.

A single "thank you"
can open a thousand doors
that effort alone
couldn't budge.

4.

What you appreciate,
appreciates.

5.

Even in the ache,
say thank you—
for the lesson,
for the strength,
for the fire
that shapes gold.

6.
Gratitude turns delays
into divine timing.

7.
Every breath you take
was once someone's final wish.
Start there.

8.
To be grateful in peace
is gentle.
To be grateful in pain—
that's alchemy.

9.
You cannot feel lack
and gratitude
at the same time.

10.
Gratitude sharpens vision—
you begin to see
what was always there,
waiting to be praised.

11.
A grateful soul
is never empty.
Even silence
becomes a song.

12.
The sun rises
without being asked.
Have you thanked it yet?

13.
Gratitude doesn't require reason—
only presence.

14.
When you bless your path,
even the stones
become sacred.

15.
Gratitude is the language
angels answer in.

16.
You'll know you've grown
when you say thank you
for what once broke you.

17.
Write it.
Whisper it.
Breathe it.
Let gratitude become
your default setting.

18.

Every "thank you"
echoes in eternity.

19.

To feel joy,
notice it.
To keep joy,
honor it.

20.

Gratitude is how you say to the universe,
"I trust you."
And the universe replies,
"Then let me show you more."

The Law of Blessings

To bless is to transmit divine energy. To offer sacred energy — to uplift and awaken. Every blessing you speak is a beam of divine light sent into form. This law reminds you that when you bless others, you elevate that energy/aura. The more you live as a blessing, the more life blesses you in return.

Key concepts:

- Blessing someone sends divine light to them.
- What you bless increases — be it people, plants, homes, or yourself.
- The act of blessing uplifts both the giver and the receiver.

THE LAW OF BLESSINGS

"To bless is to transmit light. To be blessed is to receive it."

1.

A blessing is a whisper of light—
spoken from the soul
into the shape of the world.

2.

When you bless,
you become a channel
for the divine
to touch another.

3.

Raise your hand,
speak their name,
and imagine them whole—
that is enough.

4.

Every genuine blessing
plants a seed
of peace.

5.

You can bless a wound.
You can bless a storm.

Even sorrow softens
when bathed in light.

6.
Say:
"Bless this moment."
And watch how it listens.

7.
Bless your food,
your work,
your words—
they will rise
in vibration.

8.
What you bless
begins to blossom.

9.
A home filled with blessings
becomes a temple.

10.
Bless the stranger
you may never meet—
your light still reaches them.

11.
To bless is to create a bridge
between your heart
and the divine.

12.
Bless your past.
Yes, all of it—
even the pain
that became your teacher.

13.
When you bless,
you also receive.
Light flows
in both directions.

14.
You can bless with words.
You can bless with touch.
But the greatest blessings
flow through presence.

15.
Bless your body
and it begins to remember
its sacredness.

16.

A child that is blessed
walks taller.
So does the soul.

17.

If you want more beauty
in the world,
bless what is already beautiful.

18.

Bless not just what is good—
but what is growing.

19.

Your blessing travels
faster than doubt
and deeper than fear.

20.

To bless
is to borrow the voice of grace
and offer it to the world.

The Law of Decree

A decree is a spiritual command — not a plea. It is a clear, one-time statement of divine truth that realigns your reality. Unlike affirmations or prayers, decrees align you with immediate universal response. This law teaches that when your will aligns with higher will/greater good, your voice carries authority. Decree with certainty, and the universe moves accordingly. Speak with authority, clarity, and alignment to enact this law.

Key concepts:

- A decree is a one-time, sacred command backed by full faith.
- Unlike affirmations, decrees are non-negotiable spiritual declarations.
- Only use for the highest good — they align divine will with spoken word.

THE LAW OF DECREE

"When spoken with truth and alignment, your words become law."

1.

A decree is not a hope.
It is a declaration
rooted in knowing.

2.

You do not repeat a decree.
You release it once—
and the universe begins to build.

3.

When the soul speaks firmly,
creation listens.

4.

A decree is not shouted—
it is spoken
with sacred certainty.

5.

Say:
"By divine decree,
I claim peace."
And peace will seek
its way to you.

6.

Decree is not wishful.
It is intentional.
It is encoded with clarity.

7.

The voice of decree
does not tremble.
It remembers.

8.

To decree is to plant truth
into the structure of reality.

9.

Before the mountains moved,
there was a word.

10.

What you say
with unwavering conviction
rearranges matter.

11.

A decree bypasses fear.
It carries divine authority.

12.

Decree with humility,
not pride.

For what you command
must serve the highest good.

13.
Even time bends
when the soul
makes a true decree.

14.
When your will aligns
with divine purpose,
your voice becomes
an instrument of light.

15.
Decrees dissolve old contracts—
and write new ones in light.

16.
Speak not from desperation,
but from spiritual stature.

17.
The universe answers
not just *what* you say,
but *who* you are
as you say it.

18.
A sacred "It is done"
echoes through the unseen
like thunder.

19.
Decree is the tool
of the awakened soul—
sharp, still, and unstoppable.

20.
One decree spoken in truth
can undo lifetimes
of forgetting.

The Law of Faith

Faith is knowing without needing proof. It is the certainty that divine order is always working, even in silence. This law teaches that faith magnetizes miracles and stabilizes your vibration during doubt. With faith, you walk before the path appears — and the path forms beneath your feet.

Key concepts:

- Faith is certainty beyond proof; it transcends doubt and opens divine flow.
- Fear blocks; faith activates the unseen.
- Miracles, healing, and success flow through this unwavering trust.

THE LAW OF FAITH

"Faith is the frequency that opens the invisible gate."

1.
Faith begins
where proof ends.

2.
It's not blind—
it sees farther
than the eyes can reach.

3.
When fear says, "What if?"
faith says, "Even so."

4.
To hold faith
is to hold a vibration
higher than your circumstances.

5.
Faith doesn't beg.
It walks forward
as if the bridge is already there.

6.
It is not loud—
but it is steady.
A quiet anchor
in deep waters.

7.
You don't need to believe
all day.
Just enough
to open the gate.

8.
Faith is not pretending.
It is choosing the highest truth
before it's visible.

9.
What you have faith in,
you feed with light.

10.
Doubt builds walls.
Faith builds doors.

11.
Even when shaking,
you can speak in faith—
and life will hear the deeper note.

12.
You do not need
the whole plan.
Faith begins
with one step.

13.
Faith is your soul's memory
speaking louder
than your mind's fear.

14.
You are not waiting
for the universe—
it is waiting
for your belief to solidify.

15.
To walk by faith
is to trust the soil
under a sky you've never seen.

16.
The most miraculous acts
began
with one quiet "yes."

17.

Faith is action
that makes no sense
until the miracle comes.

18.

You don't get what you wish for.
You get what you hold
through darkness.

19.

Where there is faith,
the impossible
shrinks.

20.

Faith is the vibration
where heaven and earth
agree.

The Law of Grace

Grace is love that flows without condition — a divine override that softens karma, heals wounds and accelerates healing. You cannot earn it, only receive it. This law reminds you that grace visits where there is humility, compassion, and readiness. The more compassion you extend to others, the more grace flows to you. This law is the universe's greatest kindness.

Key concepts:

- Grace is divine mercy that overrides karma when the soul is ready.
- It is accessed through compassion, forgiveness, and love.
- Offering grace to others invokes grace in your own life.

THE LAW OF GRACE

"Grace is love that arrives unearned, but never undeserved."

1.
Karma keeps the balance.
Grace tips the scale
toward mercy.

2.
Grace is what flows in
when the soul
has finally softened.

3.
You cannot earn grace.
But you can open to it.

4.
It arrives
not because you are perfect,
but because you are willing
to be real.

5.
Grace does not erase karma—
it transforms the path
into light.

6.

Where there is forgiveness,
grace waits
with open arms.

7.

Grace is divine timing
wrapped in gentleness.

8.

You do not summon grace.
You prepare a space
for it to land.

9.

Sometimes grace is a person.
Sometimes,
a pause.

10.

Grace whispers:
"You are loved,
even here."

11.

It comes not to reward,
but to uplift.

12.
One act of compassion
calls in lifetimes
of grace.

13.
The more you offer it,
the more it fills you.

14.
You know grace is near
when peace arrives
before the answer.

15.
Grace makes the heavy
light again.

16.
It follows humility
like a shadow.

17.
When you stop punishing yourself,
grace sees room
to enter.

18.

Grace does not shout.
It slips in
like dawn.

19.

You are not waiting
for grace.
You are remembering
you are worthy of it.

20.

To live in grace
is to become
a sanctuary for others.

The Law of One / Oneness

Separation is an illusion. There is no *other* — all is one. Every being, plant, moment, and experience is part of the same Source. When you live in unity consciousness, duality dissolves. Beneath all forms and faces, there is only one energy — one Source expressing itself infinitely. This law invites you to drop judgment, dissolve hierarchy, and walk in reverence. When you truly see the divine in all, peace becomes your natural state. This law is the foundation of harmlessness, peace, and unconditional love.

Key concepts:

- All is one — humans, animals, plants, Earth, and Source are inseparable.
- Judgment dissolves when you see divinity in all.
- Harmlessness, unity, and unconditional love are the highest truths.
- Understanding the concept of "Oneness of life and environment".
- Duality (light/dark, good/bad) is a temporary illusion of the Earth plane. Beyond the fifth dimension, only Oneness exists.
- Even "negative" people/situations serve us; all are part of the divine whole.
- We are all here to co-evolve, share space respectfully, and act with **harmlessness**.

THE LAW OF ONE / ONENESS

"There is no other. There never was."

1.

The tree is not outside you.
Nor the bird,
nor the man you fear.
All of it
is you
meeting itself again.

2.

There is no "them."
There is only you,
dressed differently.

3.

Even the ant
has a soul.
And that soul
is stitched
from the same light
as yours.

4.

Separation is an illusion
woven by fear.
Love

remembers
the thread beneath.

5.
To honor all things
as divine
is not naivety—
it is mastery.

6.
When you harm another,
you dim your own flame.
When you bless them,
your light expands.

7.
Beyond the veil,
there are no sides.
Only source
recognizing itself
in infinite form.

8.
You are the river,
the thirst,
and the sky it reflects.

9.
What you reject
in another
is what you have not yet
embraced in yourself.

10.
Oneness is not sameness.
It is sacred difference
held in unity.

11.
The Earth breathes you.
And you breathe her.
You've never truly been apart.

12.
Each soul,
no matter how broken,
carries a shard
of the original flame.

13.
God lives
not in temples alone—
but in every pair of eyes
you've ever looked away from.

14.
To live in oneness
is to walk gently,
speak kindly,
and remember constantly.

15.
Do not ask,
"Is this worthy of love?"
Ask,
"Can I see the One
that never left it?"

16.
Your healing
heals the whole.
Every release
sends ripples.

17.
The soul does not compete.
It collaborates.
It merges.
It remembers.

18.
Even shadow
is part of the divine.
It teaches contrast
so the light can sing.

19.

Oneness is not a goal.
It is a fact
you forgot
when you took a name.

20.

When you finally see no difference
between self and other—
peace begins.

Closing Note

If these words have reached your heart, it is because your soul was ready to remember.

You are not separate. Not different. Not behind.
You are a vital note in the song of the whole — a vibration the universe cannot sing without.

As you return to your life, may you walk with awareness. May you speak with love. May you bless all beings, including yourself. And may you remember, again and again:

You are the light.
You are the law.
You are the one.

Thank you for walking this path with me. The world is already better because you have.

Love,
Shreeya

About the Author

Shreeya Sharma is a seeker, and practitioner of sacred design. With roots in Vedic wisdom and a deep reverence for natural order, her work explores the intersection of energy, space, and the soul. Through architecture, poetry, and spiritual inquiry, she curates spaces — both inner and outer — where beauty and awareness meet. This book is not just a reflection of her path, but an offering to yours.

She lives and creates in harmony with the rhythms of the Earth, believing that when we realign with truth, life becomes poetry.

A Note to the Reader

If you enjoyed the verses, please consider leaving a review on Amazon or Goodreads. Your support helps indie creators like me reach more readers—and dream bigger.

www.ingramcontent.com/pod-product-compliance
Ingram Content Group UK Ltd.
Pitfield, Milton Keynes, MK11 3LW, UK
UKHW041954190726
13854UKWH00005B/1966

9 798899 619878